A Battle Manual for Christian Survival

by Leslie F. Brandt

Illustrated by Jim Cummins

Publishing House
St. Louis London

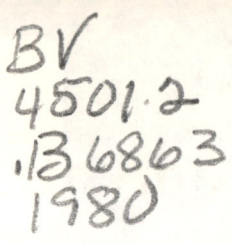

The Scripture quotations in this publication marked TEV are used by permission of American Bible Society, from the *Good News Bible,* copyright © TEV, 1966, 1971, 1976.

This book may not be reproduced in whole or in part, by mimeograph or any other means, without permission. For information address: Concordia Publishing House, St. Louis, MO 63118.

All rights reserved.
Copyright © 1980 by Concordia Publishing House

Library of Congress Cataloging in Publication Data

Brandt, Leslie F
   A battle manual for Christian survival.

   1. Christian life—1960- I. Title.
BV4501.2.B6863 1980   248.4   79-27596
ISBN 0-570-03808-1 pbk.

Contents

	Page
Preface	7
We Have the Attitudes	11
We Have the Credentials	21
We Have the Equipment	31
We Have the Ethics	41
We Have the Joy	51
We Have the Assignment	61
We Have the Methods	71
We Need the Commitment	85
On to Victory!	93

Preface

We are all—not just the doomsday prophets—living in the end-time. God reveals the fact to us in the Bible. And an unflinching look at the conditions in the world around us will confirm the possibility of the destruction of the human race. We are indeed end-time creatures.

Ever since Christ ascended into heaven after His Messianic mission on earth, the world has been living in the end-time, awaiting the Day of Judgment and Christ's return. And though millions may not live to witness that day, every human being is living in his own end-time from the moment of birth to the unknown moment of death.

No longer can the predictions and warnings of the Bible be considered mythology. Accumulating experience and observation should make all but the fool and the historically blind vividly aware of the threats to human existence on Planet Earth: nuclear proliferation, radiation, and atomic waste; pollution of the atmosphere, soil, and water; mass starvation; the inability of nations to resolve their disputes peacefully; energy blackmail; uncontrollable inflation; the dissolution of the family; rampant crime, dishonesty, and abortion; drug abuse even among children; and so on.

How does the Christian survive in such a world since he is destined to live in it? Some things he can change; others he can't. Some things can be changed simply by his living a consistent life in Christ and raising his voice against the self-destruction course of the human race. Still more things can be changed by creative and positive efforts on the part of Christians to grapple with human needs and sacrificial effort to lessen the misery of millions.

This book is not for ostriches or fools who are oblivious to life and history. It is for the concerned follower of Christ, who has taken up his cross after his Master, and who has been placed and left in this world for a purpose greater than mere survival.

Everyone who answers the call of Christ to follow Him is His disciple. These followers are the salt of the earth. How can they keep this saltiness? How can they help to preserve the world from decay and destruction? Is there really any more important question for the followers of the eternal Word?

This is not a book for or about church leaders who draw up elaborate plans and direct the troops from behind the lines. This is a battle manual for the slogging foot soldier in the army of Jesus Christ who must contend for his or her convictions alone, often in hostile surroundings, and with nothing but the power and support of the Holy Spirit to rely on. Which, author Leslie Brandt, echoing Christ the Lord, says is enough.

To you, the dedicated but perhaps faltering disciple of the living and coming Lord, these pages are offered for inspiration, encouragement, and commendation. Keep the faith!

We Have the Attitudes

Luke 12:49-56
John 16:1-4
1 Peter 4:12-19

1.

We are in the end-times of this dispensation and
    our world is beset by conflict and revolution.
It is no single revolution,
    but a whole array of revolutions:
    moral, educational, economical, political.
They are taking place in the entertainment world,
    within the arts,
    even amongst the religions that embrace this planet.
There is nothing new about revolutions.
There is no period in our history that has been
    totally free of revolutions.
Today, however, our world has shrunk.
It used to be a vast, mysterious world that we
    know very little about.
Now it is on our doorsteps every morning and in
    our living rooms every night.
We eat it for breakfast and attempt to digest it
    after dinner.

We live in a society that attempts to solve its conflicts
   with pain-killing drugs and sweet-smelling deodorants.
Our reaction to conflict or revolution is often a retreat
   to the sanctuary of the past where it is assumed
   that we can be free of the everyday tensions
   and hostilities which are associated with life
   in our present-day world.
We even look to the church where,
   "safe in the arms of Jesus,"
   we may find relief and respite from the
   frustrations of society-at-large.

Our flight from these frightening changes and events
   is totally contrary to the temper of the Gospel.
It seriously jeopardizes and,
   if Christians persist in it,
   could ultimately destroy the concept of the church.
Conflicts and revolutionary changes are even a
   necessary projection and consequence of the Gospel.
Our Lord Himself initiates the conditions that
   so often perpetuate such.
"I have come to set fire to the earth," Jesus said,
   "and how I wish it were already kindled! . . .
   Do you suppose I came to establish peace on earth?
   No, indeed, I have come to bring division"
   (Luke 12:49-52 NEB).
What He promised took place—even within His own family.
And it has affected families and churches
   and whole societies from that time until this.

We are living in the end-times of this dispensation.
We must find our place in this period of time
   as God's children and servants.
We are to live the kind of lives that will serve
   His purposes.

2.

"Peace is My parting gift to you, My own peace,
    such as the world cannot give," said Jesus.
"Set your troubled hearts at rest, and banish your fears"
    (John 14:27 NEB).
And yet the peace of Christ is in itself
    the very instigator of conflict and revolution.
We have for too long been reveling in our
    Sunday school portrayals of our Lord
    as a gentle, meek peacemaker,
        when a more honest review of His life and teachings
        portray Him as a radical and a revolutionary.
Jesus was a true radical.
He always got to the root of things.
When our Lord dealt with the poor, the ill,
    the simple-minded and the sinner,
    the publican and the fisherman,
    He spoke the words of peace and promise.
When He addressed the uptight, sanctimonious,
    hypocritical establishment of His day,
    He spoke like a revolutionary.
His words were like fire,
    burning into the hides of those oppressive and
    self-centered leaders like acid into fine silk.
As with so many great people throughout our history
    who dared to say it as it is,
    the consequence was division,
    persecution, imprisonment, and ignoble death.

Revolutions and conflicts are necessary to
    our very existence.
They have the potential of becoming violent—
    and the history of our world is permeated
    with the violence that accompanies such insurrections.

The King's Library

They have, as well, the potential of being constructive
    and often result in strength and growth.
Revolutions, cataclysmic changes, upheavals
    of one sort or another,
    have always been with us,
    and until our great God winds up history as we know it,
    they shall always be with us.
We cannot any more avoid or ignore
    these disturbing events
    than did our Lord and His faithful followers
    in the face of Judah's harlotry or Rome's paganism.
Our responsibility is to put our reputations, jobs, incomes,
    even our lives on the line to confront violence
    with courage and hatred with love.

3.

Jesus knew full well what His followers would face.
He had come to "cast fire upon the earth."
He promised that "peace that passes understanding."
He promised, as well,
    that those who labored for His kingdom would
    face division, conflict, persecution, and rebellion.
He led the way to the scaffold.
Most of His disciples followed closely behind.
And He has left us with the assuring Word that
    we need not be afraid when we face the courts
    that seek to snuff us out.
He has gone that way before us,
    but only to return in order to embrace us and love us
    in the midst of these earth-shaking events,
    and to stay close beside us all the way.

The Christian life itself is a revolutionary life—
    and a life full of conflicts.
It has been this way from the beginning;
    it shall be as long as this world continues.
Those people who float peacefully by,
    oblivious or impervious to the conflict-ridden
    world about them,
        desperately holding on to their precious ecstasies
        or god-in-a-box concepts until Jesus comes
        to take them to heaven,
    those people are on the wrong ship—
    or are stuck in some dull and decadent harbor
    when they should be sailing the high and
    storm-tossed seas of reality where God's servants
    and fishers-of-men are supposed to be.

I remember that incident when our Lord and His
    disciples were crossing the sea in a small boat.
A storm broke and the waves began washing into
    their little vessel.
While Jesus was sleeping,
    the disciples became panicky and screamed out
    to Jesus to do something lest they drown.
Awakening from His slumber, Jesus commanded the storm
    to abate and there was dead calm.
Then He said to His disciples,
    "Where is your faith?"

Our world, country, communities, even our churches,
    are tossing about on tempestuous seas.
And it appears as if the storm will get much worse
    before it gets better.
In the midst of all this we are often like those
    disciples, panic-stricken, frightened out of our wits,
    beating the air for something to cling to.
I think Christ is saying to us what He said
    to those disciples:

"Why are you such cowards?
How little faith you have!
I have created, redeemed, and appointed you
for just such times as these.
I am always with you, indwelling you,
empowering you, working out My will through you.
Trust Me; I won't let you go.
There is a quiet harbor somewhere at the end
of your journey, but for now you are to abide
in Me and to work for Me in the midst of storm."

4.

The world appears to be erupting about us.
An alien culture is swiftly displacing the one in
 which we had our roots.
Change is avalanching upon us,
 and we are not prepared to cope with it.
In the past the pace was leisurely;
 cultural changes stretched out over
 hundreds of years.
Today time is compressed.
We can witness a thousand years of change
 in a few brief decades.

How do we respond to this frightening development?
We can blindly deny its existence.
We can reach back into history for verities and
 securities and try to impose them upon others.
We can attempt to block out reality by proclaiming
 that which was valid in our years of experience.
We can continue to grope for a little nostalgia.
We can bury our heads in the sand like an ostrich

and refuse to accept the reality
of what is going on about us.
We can lash out against those spiritual leaders
who try to lead us in confronting it.
We can find refuge in a simplistic, emotional,
get-the-people-ready-for-heaven Gospel,
or ignore present-day actualities by concentrating
on the imminent second coming of Christ.
But this may render us virtually incapable
of effectual living in today's world.
We could hardly become the kind of disciples that can
represent and communicate the true Christ
and the total Gospel and carry out
His purposes in our kind of world.

As Christians, we need not fear change.
We have been set free from ancient formulas
or customs or modes of living.
We are the children of eternity.
We do not have to be afraid of what is transpiring
about us or shocked by the sweeping events
of this day in which we live.
We must sometimes roll with the punch—
to adjust, to adapt, and to respond in God-fearing,
neighbor-loving ways to whatever happens
on our course through life.
But we don't have to be afraid.
We are the objects of God's eternal, ever-present love.
And we are His servants assigned to minister
to our kind of world and to His creatures within it.

We Have the Credentials

**Romans 8:12-17
1 Corinthians 6:19-20**

1.

It is a disturbing and challenging assignment—
    to be a Christian in these end-times.
Before we can accept such an assignment,
    we must find out who we are.
A songwriter screams out his loneliness in the words:
    "Who am I, to sit and wonder, to wait,
    While the wheels of fate slowly grind my life away?
    Who am I?"
It is not only youth who are wrestling
    with identity crises;
    it is the persistent struggle of most Christians.

Those first followers of Jesus found their identity.
"You know that your bodies are parts of the body of Christ,"
    said Paul.
"Don't you know that your body is the temple
    of the Holy Spirit,
    who lives in you and who was given to you by God?

You do not belong to yourselves but to God;
   He bought you for a price"
   (1 Corinthians 6:15, 19-20 TEV).
"We are called God's children—
   and so, in fact, we are," writes John.
"My dear friends, we are now God's children"
   (1 John 3:1-2 TEV).

"You did not chose Me; I chose you," said Jesus.
I "appointed you to go and bear much fruit . . ."
   (John 5:16 TEV).
At another time Paul wrote:
"Those who are led by God's Spirit are God's sons.
For the Spirit that God has given you
   does not make you slaves and cause you to be afraid;
   instead, the Spirit makes you God's children,
   and by the Spirit's power we cry out to God,
   'Father! my Father!'
God's Spirit joins Himself to our spirits
   to declare that we are God's children.
Since we are His children,
   we will possess the blessings He keeps for His people,
   and we will also possess with Christ
   what God has kept for Him;
   for if we share Christ's suffering,
   we will also share His glory" *(Romans 8:14-47 TEV).*

They apparently had little trouble with identity,
   those first disciples of our Lord.
They took Jesus at His word and,
   despised by the Romans and hated by their own people,
   they purposefully dedicated their lives to
   carrying out His commission—
   most of them paying the price of violent death
   in their commitment to God and His purposes.
They knew who they were and where they were going.
Their real citizenship was in a world beyond this one.

They were on a mission for their Lord.
Everything else was of secondary importance.

We became God's heirs, His very children,
    through our baptism.
In that significant happening,
    the Spirit of the living God entered
    our hearts and lives.
Now we know who we are and to whom we belong and,
    ultimately, if not presently, where we are going.

———— 2. ————

Pastors, pressed by their denominational superiors,
    judge success in terms of membership
    and budget statistics.
Writers strive to get their names on provocative
    articles or bestselling books.
Artists seek out admiring fans.
And I confess that plaudits and commendations are
    inordinately important to me.
If judged by such standards,
    our Lord was one of the most fantastic flops of history.
He preached and miraculously fed 5,000 people,
    but only a handful remained to follow Him.
He was "hosanna'd" by palm-branch-waving multitudes,
    and mourned by a few women
    when He was executed a few days later.

If we are out to create a popular religion,
    we do well to package our Lord in Madison Avenue,

mass-media methods and sell Him the way our society
sells politicians to a gullible public.
If we are committed to this Christ and His objectives—
that of revealing God's reconciling
and redeeming love to out-of-orbit humankind—
it may very well take us down the unpopular path
of persecution and may even earn for us
the dubious status of misguided martyrs.

Discipleship is, indeed, a hard road.
And it will not be lined with cheerleaders or fans
egging us on to the finish line.
Our Lord does place refreshing oases along our paths—
usually in the most unsuspecting places—
strangers that are angels unawares,
beautiful people who will love us
with no strings attached,
even some indefinable ecstatic experience
that refurbishes and restores
the original glow of our spiritual convictions.
When these oases, however, become the object
of our travels through life,
they are seldom discovered—
or even recognized when they appear.
Many have been trapped by
some such green spot on the road,
have shriveled up into little self-centered cults,
and never proceeded beyond into the real business of
Christ's assigned tasks of loving, serving,
and relating God to humanity.

As for us, we must get on with the job,
whether it takes us to mountaintop or valley,
and "share His sufferings now in order to share
His splendor hereafter."

3.

When our Lord proclaimed that His followers
 would be doing greater things than that
 which He exemplified before them,
 He meant it—and He was also speaking about us.
He was, of course, referring to those
 who would truly follow Him,
 who would dedicate themselves to His principles
 and commit their lives to the
 accomplishment of His purposes.
He did not mean that they or we would be performing miracles
 or exorcising demons in exactly the same way He did.
Nevertheless, what Christ began,
 His disciples would continue in ever-increasing measure
 until the whole world would know about God's love.

This certainly means that Christ's brothers and
 sisters are very special people—
 God's special people to whom He has entrusted the job
 of carrying on the incarnation of Jesus Christ.
Jesus did what human beings could not do in making
 a way of salvation for God's beloved creatures.
We are commissioned and empowered to do what Jesus
 cannot do in relating His redemptive love
 to the 20th-century inhabitants of this planet.

"He who receives you receives Me," Jesus once said,
 "and he who receives Me receives Him who sent me"
 (Matthew 10:40 RSV).
Jesus makes Himself as dependent upon today's disciples
 as God made Himself dependent upon Jesus.
This is what the incarnation is all about.
God's children in our century are the only means He has

of reaching the humanity of our century.
That is how special we are—and we are responsible
for discovering 20th-century means of doing the job.

It was somewhere in the midst of his contemplations about
creation and the human condition that David once gasped,
"Thou hast made him little less than a god,
crowning him with glory and honor" *(Psalm 8:5 NEB)*.
It is through the eyes of the New Testament that we can
see the why and wherefore of this glorious truth.
When Moses inquired as to the identity of God,
the answer he received was: "I AM; that is who I am"
(Exodus 3:14 NEB).
Reconciled to God through Christ,
we must recognize who we are, and acquire the insight
to state with confidence and conviction,
"We are the brothers and sisters of Christ,
and the children and servants of God."

The human creature is born with an inferiority complex.
He or she spends the better part of life
seeking to overcome it,
to discover worth and validity,
often through bizarre ways that only drive one
further from the Creator.
Through Christ we have been restored to God's orbit,
reunited to God's family and kingdom.
We have been adopted as God's sons and daughters,
chosen to be Christ's disciples,
and committed to the eternal purposes of the
heavenly Father.
These are our credentials.
They make us very special indeed.

We Have the Equipment

**John 13:25-31; John 17
Acts 2:14-21
2 Peter 1:3-4**

1.

Having considered our credentials as God's children
    and servants assigned to live and serve
    in the end-times,
    we need to discover, to acknowledge,
    to learn how to use our equipment.
Peter once wrote:
    "His divine power has given us everything we need to
    live a truly religious life through our knowledge of the One
    who called us to share in His own glory and goodness"
    (2 Peter 1:3 TEV).
He was writing this to a group of people who had suffered
    much and who expected to suffer much more in the
    world that they encountered.
They wondered whether they had what it took to face
    the kind of world that closed in about them.

I have seriously questioned my capabilities in respect
    to my assignment in these end-times.

In a world of computers and space shuttles and laser beams,
    of status-quo, country-club religious institutions,
    of rebellious youth and oppressed minorities,
    of atheistic ideologies and facist political philosophies,
    a world that could be destroyed instantly with
    a push-button war,
    or gradually become extinct through the continued
    misuse and abuse of its natural resources,
    a world that appears to be on the brink
    of a great and violent revolution,
    my first inclination is to burrow into some deep,
    dark hole and pull it in after me.
My natural faculties simply do not enable me
    to face this kind of a world.
I admit to fear as well as frustration,
    to an agonizing feeling of emptiness and inadequacy.
I am tempted, in my more desperate moments,
    to join one of those cults that await Christ's
    imminent return or God's ultimate windup of history.
I would like to ignore the frightening things
    taking place in the world about me,
    to avoid the Great Tribulation,
    and focus upon the rather vague proposal
    that I can be miraculously delivered
    from the obscene consequences of humankind's
    selfishness and Satan's deviousness and,
    even without the troublesome event of death,
    be transported to the eternal, joyful, peaceful,
    blissful home in the sky—
    while the world behind me goes to hell.

That day may come—tomorrow—or a decade from now.
But we are here—and now.
We are credentialed—appointed and commissioned—
    for just such a time as this.
"His divine power has given us everything we need
    to live a truly religious life . . ."

How do we go about accepting it, laying claim to it—
    how can we make it work in and through our lives?

2.

It is difficult to imagine how people can die
    of malnutrition with hundred-dollar bills stuffed
    into their mattresses.
And yet it happens from time to time.
It is a common enough malady amongst many Christians.
While God stands by to provide all that is needed to
    live effective, contributive, joy-filled lives,
    His children are struggling
    with spiritual malnutrition.
Maybe it isn't often verbalized,
    but religious and not-so-religious people often
    question God's apparent limitations
    in our chaotic world today.

God is indeed limited—
    primarily by the unbelief of His children and
    their unwillingness to take Him as His Word.
He has no hands but our hands,
    and when they hang limp with unbelief
    or rigid with fear,
    they are hardly active in creating or healing
    or carrying out the purposes of God.
Thus the body of Christ is crippled and the world
    impoverished through the timidity
    or the faithlessness of His own servants.

Most of us don't have much trouble with Christmas,
    but Pentecost is still one colossal mystery.

We are quite comfortable with the manger scene,
    even with Calvary's cross,
    and especially with Easter and its grand tidings
    of victory over sin and death—
    but Pentecost is something totally incomprehensible
    for many of us.

Of course there must be Christmas, Good Friday, and
    Easter experiences in our lives,
    but this is to prepare the way for Pentecost.
Pentecost is the culmination of everything
    that went before it.
It is the key to God's invisible presence
    and power in our world today.
If we are to manifest His presence and project His power,
    we, too, must be the product of Pentecost.

3.

Some Christians are still waiting for Pentecost to happen.
They identify it with a second blessing, a special baptism,
    or the same signs and symbols that marked
    the Holy Spirit's takeover
    of some of those first-century disciples.
And some people apparently receive what they
    so intensely seek—
    an ecstatic, hair-raising, soul-shaking experience
    that turns them on and pushes them out
    into this revolutionary world to fearlessly confront the
    enemies of God with the radical Gospel of Jesus Christ.

It is not our prerogative to deny or defy
    the experience of another.

There is room for all sorts of phenomena
   in God's scheme of things.
It may well be that people are incapable
   of moving off dead center until some
   out-of-this world happening shakes them up.
God's Word declares very clearly, however,
   that He who called us has already equipped us
   for our role in this end-times period
   of this world's history.
Our Lord did not really depart when He appeared
   to ascend into heaven.
He simply disappeared.

God in the visible Christ had completed that part
   of His universal plan.
It was now God and Christ clothed with the mortal,
   fallible, failure-fraught bodies and spirits
   of His redeemed children
   who would carry on His plan to consummation.

In the profound prayer to His Father on behalf of
   His disciples, Jesus said:
   "I gave them the same glory You gave Me,
   so that they may be one, just as You and I are one;
   I in them and You in Me, so they may be completely one,
   in order that the world may know that You sent Me
   and that You love them as You love Me" *(John 17:22-23 TEV).*
Pentecost proved that God became flesh not only by way of
   the womb of Mary and in the earthly sojourn of Christ
   but for all time and until the end of time.
He did this by infilling, indwelling, and empowering
   the flesh of His human creatures.
His indwelling is as real in each of us
   as it was in God incarnate, Jesus Christ.
And this in spite of our fallible, failure-fraught,
   sin-ridden bodies and spirits.

4.

It is Pentecost that inaugurated the perpetual
    presence of Christ in our world—
    through us and through our fellow disciples in
    the Christian faith.
Whereas Christmas means that God became man,
    Pentecost initiates that event whereby man and woman
    become the vehicles and channels,
    the very temples of God Himself.
Under our God we are divinely infilled to represent
    and to reflect Him.
The birth of Christ took place at night
    in the seclusion of a stable.
Pentecost blazed forth in broad daylight with hundreds
    of people to witness this fantastic event.
It was no longer God becoming man,
    but a whole group of men and women
    becoming God-filled—
    the vehicles and vessels of His love and power
    to a distorted world.

The fact is, God's faithful children are the only
    "Christs" that God has to advance His kingdom and
    carry out His purposes in these end-times.
We are in the midst of conflict and revolution in order
    to continue and carry on the incarnation of God—
    that He in His love for us and through our love for
    others may communicate and demonstrate divine love
    and healing to the lonely, unloved, frightened
    and fractured people all about us.
And He has already equipped us for this very task.
Setting us free from sin's guilt and power and
    eternal consequences,
    He has given us His Spirit.
The same power that brought the visible Christ into

    our world through the virgin Mary and raised Him
    from the dead on the Day of Resurrection
    is that same power, that divine energy,
    that abides within us.
This is our equipment,
    and it is more than adequate for the task that
    our God has set before us.

We Have the Ethics

Matthew 5:38-48; 22:34-40
John 15:12-17
1 John 4

1.

The challenge of being and serving as one of the
   many incarnate Christs in our kind of world
   must include a consideration of the morality,
   the standards, the ethics
   of God's sons and daughters
   that live and serve in this world.
This is necessary particularly in view of the rather
   immature concepts of Christian morality that church
   groups have subscribed to throughout our history.
The bizarre actions of our youth culture today may be,
   in part, reactions to much of what the church
   has clung to or the moral absolutes it has
   created in the name of Christianity.
We cannot condone many of these reactions.
It is certainly important that we discover and
   demonstrate right actions in our day-by-day relations
   to our fellow beings about us.
Nor do we feel that the church's concepts of morality
   are all wrong.

Many of them, however,
  are at best very dated and incomplete.

Morality to many church members is not so much what the
  Bible promotes, but what is convenient, comfortable,
  and respectable in their particular circumstances.
Many solid church people have been programmed into
  rigid concepts of life and living that have no
  basis whatsoever as far as God's Word in concerned.
This programmed or self-induced morality becomes a sort
  of security blanket that somehow sustains them
  within a tempestuous world.
Whereas such may appear to be a defense against
  the violence and licentiousness
  that is tearing our societies apart,
  it may in some cases be one of its root causes.
It certainly makes Christianity unpalatable to scores
  of sincere truthseekers in their pursuit for
  meaning and purpose in the world today.

In view of Christ's principles and prerequisites,
  church people are not necessarily Christians.
Even authentic Christians, however,
  will not always agree on moral standards,
  but will accept and reflect what they have been
  programmed to believe through the influences
  and circumstances that have surrounded them.
How, then, in view of our role as maturing Christians
  in this end-time period of our world's history,
  should we determine our standards as
  disciples of Jesus Christ?

2.

We ought to be capable of cutting into and critically
  analyzing the programming of our past and present and

allow the Spirit of God to teach us how to live by
the original standards of morality as instituted
by God Himself.
These standards were simply and profoundly stated
by God as He related them to humankind
in the initial stages of Jewish history.
God's children were commanded to love God
with their whole beings—
and to love their neighbor as themselves.
Because they were incapable of such love—
in understanding or practice—
those standards were communicated in the form of a
number of commandments which negatively expressed
love in primitive terms of what people should not do
in their relationships to God and their fellow beings.
Jesus Christ came to set us free from slavish adherence
to manmade laws and institutions,
to redefine God's original standards,
and by His divine love to unite all of His
followers around the love-God-love-your-neighbor
absolutes that have undergirded all of
God's dealings with humanity.
He went a step further than we often care to go.
He joined the love-God and love-your-neighbor absolutes
into one single standard.
He repeatedly stated or inferred that when one
truly loves his neighbor,
he is thus fulfilling the command of loving God.

It appears that there are comparatively few in our
generation who understand Christianity in these terms.
At least some of Christ's disciples did.
"Let us love one another," wrote John,
"because love comes from God.
Whoever loves is a child of God and knows God,
for God is love . . .
God is love,

and whoever lives in love lives in union with God
and God lives in union with him. . . .
We love because God first loved us.
If someone says He loves God but hates his brother,
he is a liar.
For he cannot love God, whom he has not seen,
if he does not love his brother, whom he has seen"
(1 John 4:7-8, 16, 19-20 TEV).

The Ten Commandments are not invalid.
In the light of Christ's revelations, they are primitive.
Our standards as maturing Christians must far supersede
the Law as stated in the Old Testament.
There were many struggles amongst those first-century
Christians between the Old Testament and the
New Testament moralities,
or between those who were hung up with the ancient law
and those who had gained some insight into
the meaning of the Gospel.
Paul was probably the most enlightened and avid
interpreter of Jesus' Gospel,
and he emphatically declared that Christians
are set free from the Law in order
to accept God's love revealed through Christ
and His redemption and are enabled by His invisible
Spirit to relate in love to their fellow beings.
In other words, the Ten Commandments as the Old Testament
Israelites interpreted and added on to them
are no longer to be our goal as Christians,
nor a means of winning God's favor.
Having accepted God's free gift of love,
we must go back to the basic absolutes
of love-God-love-your-neighbor, which
can be understood and fulfilled only through faith
in, and obedience to, Jesus Christ and His teachings.
As a matter of fact, Jesus enjoined His disciples
"to love one another as I have loved you."

It is this, then, that must become our objective
and goal as Christ's disciples in these end-times.

3.

I have wondered about those very loving people who
profess no belief in Jesus Christ.
Is it possible that they are closer to God and more
accurately reflecting Him than they or I realize?
It is probable that they are closer to God than many
of those who glibly repeat creeds and confessions
Sunday after Sunday.
I imagine that one can feel very warm and loving,
even ecstatically so, toward whatever or whomever
he or she has learned or experienced to be God.
And I cannot deny or disprove that experience.
At the same time,
if it does not result in a deep compulsion to reach
out in selfless love to one's brothers and sisters,
such an experience is in question.

Our neighbor is, in a very real sense,
God's representative designed to receive our
services and sacrifices of love on God's behalf.
When we love and serve our neighbor,
we love and serve God.

There are at least two ways in which people who call
themselves Christians delude themselves
and others in respect to their status.
One has to do with those who propose or pretend to live
by the Old Testament rules of morality.
They pledge allegiance to the Golden Rule and the

Ten Commandments, but instead of adopting the
love-God-love-your-neighbor absolute that inaugurated
those rules—an absolute they know they cannot
consistently adhere to—
they put on a facade of righteousness,
create their own set of standards,
and find some satisfaction and security
in the supposition that they don't kill, steal,
or get in trouble with the police.
And this, they convince themselves,
puts them on the side of God.
While they avoid outright sexual immorality
and faithfully assume the responsibility
of taking care of their families
and keeping the law of the land,
our great God may be finding them guilty of other
immoralities—bigotry and prejudice, apathy and
indifference toward other races or towards the poor,
or of rank self-centeredness in their materialistic
clutch upon the things of this life.

On the other side of the ledger are those individuals
who pursue some kind of intensely subjective
and often ecstatic religious experience
that appears to free them from personal responsibility
toward the distortions of their society and world.
They, for most part, wall themselves up in their
personal experiences or their little
clubs-for-saints and there hope to wait out the
storm until Jesus comes to take them to heaven.
Conversion to Christ may often begin in this manner.
It all too often gives way to a kind of self-centered
ecstasy and morality that does very little
for the world about us.

It is not difficult to talk the talk that bears some
resemblance to the Christian reality.

I am discovering it to be increasingly difficult to
   walk the walk of a disciple of Christ.

4.

We are responsible to live within all laws
   and regulations that benefit humanity
   and promote human welfare and happiness.
We are equally responsible in terms of disapproving,
   changing, and in some cases, even disobeying those
   manmade laws that do not subscribe to God's absolutes
   and that do not benefit the human family.
Nevertheless, the breach of the one commandment
   to love our neighbor and thereby to love God
   is the real sin with which we need to be concerned.

The churches that insist that they proclaim
   and promote the teachings of Christ
   are sometimes doing so only in part.
Jesus took the Old Testament injunctions to love God
   and our neighbor and welded them
   into one total prerequisite for,
   and consequence of, the Christian experience.
Most of us have faithfully subscribed to the
   first table of the Law and insist that we are dedicated
   to receiving and responding to God's love.
Our catechumenal and church-member requirements are
   predicated on vows to renounce the devil and all
   his works and all his ways and to love God with all
   our hearts, souls, and bodies.
The New Testament, however,
   and this is where we often fall short,
   declares the utter impossibility of loving God—

and the difficulty of being or continuing to be
    Christians—apart from loving our fellow persons.

Immorality, as I have come to understand it,
    is the failure to love my neighbor
    even as Jesus loves me.
It is, as well, the failure to stand up against those
    inhuman institutions and laws that divide races,
    perpetuate bigotry, perpetrate injustice,
    favor the rich over against the poor,
    or that promote wars of violence that destroy the
    lives and property of other nations as well as the
    souls, if not the bodies, of our fellow citizens.

Our standards, as the children and servants of God,
    must be determined in each situation
    by what we understand and believe
    is "the most loving thing to do."
It is often ambiguous.
It means that we must be sensitive to the
    enlightenment of history,
    the expectations and requirements of our culture,
    and open always to the promptings
    of God's Spirit and the guidance of His Word.
Even then we will sometimes fail to discern between
    our neighbor's genuine need
    and our own instincts and desires.
And yet we know what must be our ultimate course,
    our inevitable goal, our day-by-day intentions.
Having received God's eternal grace,
    having become the objects of His never-ceasing love,
    we must dedicate our lives to the needs
    of our fellow beings,
    discovering in God's great love for us
    the compulsion to love our neighbor
    irregardless of the consequences for our own beings.

We Have the Joy

**John 16:20-24
Philippians 4**

1.

The effervesence and ecstasy that accompanies
   the religious experiences of some people
   is neither the promise nor the proof
   of the Christian happening.
Nor should it be.
Even if it were possible to completely overcome
   our own conflicts and failures,
   we are called upon to share or to help bear
   the pains and problems of our fellow beings.
And yet, even while the boat rocks and the earth trembles
   and the heart is beset with doubts and fears,
   there is joy—
   joy mixed with pain and sorrow and depression and defeat.
It is a joy that is often limited by our inability
   to truly and persistently embrace
   God's great gift of love and acceptance.
It is joy that is tempered by the agonies and sorrows
   of our fellow persons.
Nevertheless, it is joy profound and eternal,
   deep and lasting.

It is not self-induced,
>   or the result of some inner chemistry,
>   nor is it dependent upon a favorable set
>   of circumstances.
It is a gift of God that comes to everyone who will
>   receive it and respond to it.

Unfortunately, some of the old liturgies of the church
>   as well as the tone and temper of many worship services,
>   have often taken much of the joy
>   out of the Christian experience.
The traditional emphasis of formal worship appeared so
>   often to focus upon humankind's depravity,
>   people's sins and shortcomings, faults and failures.
We sometimes gave the impression that we rather
>   enjoy wallowing in self-pity.
The real problem, however,
>   was not and is not with liturgical formats.
They include all the elements of the Gospel—
>   confession, celebration, exhortation, communion.
It is with the attitudes of those who worship.
It sometimes appears that people would rather count
>   their sins than count their blessings.
They take to wallowing or commiserating when they ought
>   to be dancing and laughing and beating drums.
Glum, solemn worship services are often the reflection
>   of glum, solemn, deadpan lives.

The fact is,
>   commiseration ought to give way to celebration—
>   if and when people take the Gospel seriously.

——— 2. ———

There is reason for perpetual joy.
We have been set free from sin's guilt

and eternal consequences.
We have been restored to God's orbit and destiny
 for our lives.
We are His sons and daughters forever.
We belong to Him.
Even when we fail, we belong to Him,
 and He will never let us go.
There is a time for weeping and regretting—
 but not for long.
The Christian experience is one of joy—perpetual joy—
 and only when our lives and our worship services
 reflect this, will they offer any sort of attraction
 to the unhappy, joyless world about us.

It all harks back to what we really believe
 about ourselves as God's sons and daughters.
If we really love and accept ourselves as God loves
 and accepts us, it may or may not resolve in ecstasy;
 it will most certainly resolve in joy.

Regardless of the format of our worship services,
 worshiping together with our comrades in Christ
 is essential.
The beauty and splendor of formal worship experiences,
 as well as the enrichment that comes in participating
 and sharing in small groups,
 contributes so very much to the faltering Christian
 in a revolutionary world.
We need that mountaintop meditation if we are to be
 joyfully and lovingly effective in the Monday-
 through-Saturday valley of dedication and service.

God is not sitting on the altars of our churches;
 He is with us on the mountaintop or in the valley.
Nevertheless, we need the added courage and strength
 that comes through the bodies and spirits
 of others who follow the Christ.

And we need the repeated proclamation of the Word and
    participation in the Sacrament of the Altar that
    expresses that Word in a very tangible way.

The keynote, however, should be celebration.
To worship is to declare our great God's worth.
This may done with our voices and bodies,
    with whispers of awe and shouts of acclamation,
    with songs and musical instruments and cymbals and drums,
    with major chords and minor chords,
    with marches and with waltzes,
    with clapping hands and stamping feet,
    with prayers and proclamation, symbols and sacraments.

Joy and worship go together.
Joy explodes into worship.
Worship, however, is not to be confined to
    church sanctuaries.
Every day that we awaken to is a precious gift
    from a loving God.
It should be greeted with praise
    and concluded with celebration.
This does not have to be packaged in long prayers
    or solemn liturgies.
Worship isn't confined to music or words;
    it is far more adequately expressed in the
    day-by-day walk of joyous trust and obedience.

If God sees fit to trust us with the assignment of
    representing and communicating Him to the lonely,
    lost people of this broken world,

each day He gives us is a gift and a challenge
all by itself—and a sign of His loving trust
in us as His children and servants.
Our obedience, our willingness to risk all to
accomplish His purposes,
this is the kind of worship that pleases
the heart of God, and it is the kind,
with or without singing or dancing,
that truly celebrates His presence
in our world today.

Worship is a sort of ongoing conversation with God.
The Bible is essential and the prayer book helpful,
but the children of God are really never
out of contact with their Father
with or without a daily prayer ritual.
Whereas marked times for worship and prayer
are important for most Christians,
their relationship to God is not totally dependent
upon a disciplined prayer time.
God doesn't make appointments for particular
times or places.
He is with His sons and daughters whatever the
hour or the circumstances.
It may be that the primary contribution of the
disciplined ritual or prayer time
is to repeatedly impress upon and program into the mind
of a Christian the fact that God is present,
that God is aware of all his or her needs and will,
as long as the heart and mind are open and obedient,
carry out His purposes through His children.

Nor is God dependent upon our long prayers
to acquaint Him of our diverse needs.
Our prayers may not do much for God.
They may do something for us—
unless, that is, they are coverups or rationalizations
for the failure to live committed lives.

And the prayers that do the most for us are not the
   repetitious recital of our needs,
   God knows already what they are,
   but the explosions of praise for God's care and
   concern whatever the circumstances that surround us.

——— 4. ———

There are many of God's children who apparently need
   the disciplined prayer hour to keep them honest
   and upright during the day.
There are others who can effectively carry on a sort of
   running conversation with God as they labor
   within His purposes for them.
Prayer refers basically,
   not to some semantic approach to the Deity,
   but to a daily walk with God.
This is the "praying without ceasing" that Paul must
   have alluded to.
This does not rule out the prayer hour
   but suggests something even more meaningful for us—
   and even this must include, disciplined or otherwise,
   periods when, in solitude and with others, we pause to
   reflect upon and to renew our relationship of trust in,
   and love for both God and our comrades in Christ.

There is something we must learn how to do:
    it is to begin and end each day, as well as every week,
   with celebration.
It would be well if we spent less time with pious
   consideration of our failures
   and more time in celebrating the loving forgiveness
   and acceptance that God has already offered to us.
I wonder if there is anything our world is more in need of

than the honest and unrepressed joy of God's children
who truly accept God's gifts of redemption
and reconciliation and who respond to God's eternal
love by lovingly offering their bodies and beings
on the altar of their fellow person's needs.

As Christians in these end-times,
    We walk a sometimes difficult and discouraging path.
There are moments of ecstasy—
    a Pacific sunset, a Bach chorale,
    a Beethoven symphony, a walk in the woods,
    a conversation with a dear friend.
There are hours of pain and frustration—
    our own defeats, our friend's suffering,
    our unmet or assumed needs,
    our apparently unfruitful endeavors.
But through it all there is joy—
    deep, profound, inexplicable joy.
It is the joy of knowing that we are God's children,
    God's servants, that all that is His is ours,
    and that we are His forever.

We Have the Assignment

Matthew 28:16-20
Luke 10:25-37

1.

There once was a lawyer who wanted to know how
   he could be sure of heaven.
"What does the Law say?" asked Jesus of the lawyer.
"You shall love the Lord your God with all your heart,
   and with all your soul, and with all your strength,
   and with all your mind; and your neighbor as yourself,"
   responded the lawyer.
"That is correct," said Jesus.
"Do this and heaven is guaranteed."
This lawyer was not about to challenge the old and
   revered commandment,
   but he was as cagy as the best of us and probably more
   honest than most of us in posing the question,
   "And who is my neighbor?"

I don't know if our Lord's answer was a surprise
   to the lawyer, but His recital of the parable
   of the Good Samaritan is a revealing and judgmental

condemnation upon much that goes under the name
of Christianity today.
The lawyer knew that no human being could challenge
his love for God.
After all, he said the right words.
He went through the required motions.
He carried on a very respectable kind of life.
But the second half of the commandment—
love of neighbor—stopped him cold.
That was where the authenticity of his faith
could be challenged.
And he had only one recourse: "Who is my neighbor?"

It is this, the story of the Good Samaritan,
that tends to make so much of our professed and assumed
piety appear to be something less than authentic.
Of course, salvation is God's gift.
It cannot be earned or merited.
It must be accepted as God's gift as demonstrated and
proclaimed by Jesus Christ.
We can't earn a love that is already granted.
We can only accept it—or refuse or neglect to accept it.
It is when we truly and authentically embrace it
that we become channels and communicators
of divine love toward our neighbor.
Nevertheless, in our emphasis upon the
subjective experience,
the personal relationship to Christ,
and upon getting people to confess their sins
and declare their faith in Jesus Christ as their Savior,
we have often neglected the second great precept
of a vital and valid Christianity,
the other side of the Gospel coin—
our relationship to our neighbor.

This may very well be the reason some of us
are reluctant to face the import of the
"love-your-neighbor" aspect of the Great Commandment.

It challenges the profession or expression of our
   faith and reveals the authenticity or phoniness
   of our religious beliefs.

2.

As long as we say the right words and belong
   to the right church,
   our faith can't be proved or disproved by mortal man.
The parable of the Good Samaritan, however,
   pins us up against the wall and demands that
   we "put up" or "shut up."

We recognize the charge and the need to proclaim the Gospel
We have invested money and talents in the great task of
   bringing the Gospel of Jesus Christ to the whole world.
If we ever cease preaching Christ and His power to save
   and the people's need to embrace Him as Savior,
   we had better demit and begin selling something useful—
   like encyclopedias or insurance.
On the other hand,
   those people who assume the command to "love their
   neighbor" can be fulfilled by preaching,
   reciting Scripture, sending Bibles, or even praying a lot,
   should try this concept on their mates or children
   or dear friends to see just how far they get.
Is it any wonder that the displaced, deprived,
   oppressed and poverty-stricken masses of our world
   fail to respond to this limited kind of a witness?

There is no question whatsoever about the why and
   whatfor of our salvation.
It comes from God; it comes as a gift.

It is not enough, however, to say the right words like,
    "I love You, Jesus," or, "I accept You, Christ."
There must be a total committal,
    a placing of ourselves at God's disposal,
    the presentation of our bodies as living sacrifices.
This is not mere words; it is an act.
And the only way that we can really act in this manner
    toward the invisible God is to commit ourselves
    to the needs of our visible neighbor.

The "love-your-neighbor" absolute
    does not make us humanists.
The non-Christian who truly loves his or her fellow beings
    must be doing so by the grace of God
    even if he or she is not aware of it.
Though our great God may accomplish some of His great
    purposes through this person,
    the humanist works from a different premise and can
    hardly be aware of the joy and enrichment of abiding
    within God's orbit and order for his or her life.
Until we have enough genuine Christians to keep our
    world from falling apart,
    we had better not berate the humanists.
However, the Christian's motivation for loving one's
    fellow beings is God and His love.
The command to love and the ability to love are directly
    from God—and he or she is responsible to God.
This will make this person,
    assuming that he or she is truly committed,
    a far more genuine lover, and ultimately,
    a more effective lover than those humanist friends.
And the Christian's ultimate goal is to relate people
    to their Creator and Redeemer even though the
    initial approach to one's neighbor may deal
    almost entirely with that person's human needs.

3.

Who is our neighbor?
Our Lord gave the answer—loud and clear.
Every human being is our neighbor—
    and this without regard to color or background
    or social status.
Christ's overall command to the church is to preach
    the Gospel to every creature.
The personal requirement for every Christian is to
    love his or her fellow being.
And if we think this is overemphasized or exaggerated,
    we need only listen to what God's Word declares:
    "The man without love for his brother is living
    in death already," writes John.
And this is true regardless of how much Scripture
    that man quotes, how often he prays,
    or how much he gives to his favorite charity.

Who is our neighbor?
Those lonely senior citizens in rest homes
    throughout our communities,
    deserted wives with children under their feet
    and mother-Hubbard cupboards,
    the couple breaking up next door,
    the black family over on X Street,
    the minority-race people who just moved in on Y Avenue,
    the teenagers who smoke pot and steal hubcaps
    within a stone's throw of the church,
    the refugees of Vietnam—
    these are our neighbors.
And God's command is that we love them—
    not with sentimental or dutiful words,
    but with Christ-impelled actions.

How do we fulfill our Lord's command to love them?
It was John the baptizer who emerged from the wilderness
    to prepare the people for Christ's appearance.
He blasted away at the crowd with severe denunciations
    of their hypocrisy and fruitlessness.
They had faithfully performed their religious exercises
    and proudly clung to their traditions.
According to the baptizer, however,
    they had about as much chance of becoming a part
    of God's kingdom as a dead fruit tree had
    of escaping the axe.
They were stripped naked under his scathing condemnations.
"Then what are we to do?" they exclaimed.
John's reply was simple and to the point:
    "The man with two shirts
    must share with him who has none."
When Jesus concluded the Good Samaritan parable,
    He referred to the three men who had been confronted
    with the man who was beaten and robbed
    and asked the lawyer,
        "Which of these three do you think proved neighbor
        to the man who fell among the robbers?"
"The one who showed mercy on him," responded the lawyer.
And Jesus said to him, "Go and do likewise."

4.

"Go and do likewise."
Maybe this is a rather simplistic approach to the
    meaning of love,
    but this is usually where it begins.
And this, in essense, is what Jesus is saying
    to His church in these end-times.

Some people may call it the social gospel,
> but we have it on good authority that it is an
> important part of the Gospel of Jesus Christ.

"Go and do likewise."
This is our assignment.
We are to do it through our denominational structures
> that can and do reach out to the needs of masses
> of people throughout the world.

We are to do it through social and political agencies that
> through mental health, educational, and welfare projects
> touch the needs of people in our crowded cities.

We are to do it through our congregations that can zero in
> on specific needs in communities such as
> nursery schools and youth centers and care programs.

We are to do it through the personal touch where we can
> reach out in love to others around us.

Through our love, inspired and empowered by God's love,
> we can hopefully and ultimately introduce people
> to the redeeming love of Jesus Christ.

We can well afford to worry less about our personal
> salvation, our personal security or peace of mind,
> and become more concerned about responding
> to God's grace.

He has taken care of our salvation.
Heaven, whatever and wherever that may be,
> is our eventual destiny.

In the meantime,
> God has a job for us to carry out in this
> fractured world—the Good Samaritan task
> of loving our neighbor and of dramatizing
> that love at the point of his or her immediate need.

"Go and do likewise!"

We Have
the Methods

**Matthew 25:31-46
Luke 10:1-9
1 Peter 2:9**

―――― **1.** ――――

We must understand that Jesus Christ has called us,
    not to salvation alone, but to servanthood.
The church has taken great pains to assert that
    justification is by faith,
    that grace is not merited but must be received.
Perhaps it has failed to adequately present and promote
    the other side of the coin—
    that God's grace bestowed upon us results
    in transforming us into ministers and servants of God.

In other words, we are not called and redeemed by God
    in order to pull out of this sinful world,
    to be washed off and shined up and put on display
    before the masses, who are already fed up with the
    sight and sound of a dormant or verbal piety;
    but we are called and redeemed and empowered
    for the very purpose of carrying on
    the incarnation of Jesus Christ,
    of going directly into the world,

its sewers and cesspools, its sickness and distortions,
its emptiness and ugliness,
and there to show and tell God's love and Christ's
salvation and the Holy Spirit's presence and power.
And we are to do this, not primarily as preachers,
but as the servants of God.

Every one of God's sons and daughters,
Christ's sisters and brothers,
has been endowed with this gigantic responsibility
of being ministers and servants.
A servant receives his call and takes
his orders from God.
His first concern is his personal relationship to God.
Thus he worships and communes with God—
by himself and in fellowship with other
ministers and servants.
The servant also focuses her gifts and energies
in service to humankind.
What she has received from God she has received
not only for herself but for ministering
to others in her path.
A servant, or disciple, is one, or one of the many,
who carries the power and purposes of God into
every phase and facet of society—
to the rich and the poor, labor and management,
illiterate and educated,
and who represents God and speaks and ministers
for God in the industrial, commercial, governmental,
educational, scientific, economic, political,
medical, racial complexes of society.
A true disciple is one who demonstrates and makes
applicable and relevant God's love for humanity through
one-by-one relationships that personalize that love
in very genuine responses to the person next door,
the coworker at the office, the cantankerous boss,
the crabby neighbor, a sick relative, a hungry child.

A disciple of Christ is one who identifies with the
    person or persons he or she ministers to,
    who literally gives of himself or herself lovingly
    and sacrificially in order to share or to bear
    the pains and problems of others.
A disciple, or minister, is one who recognizes that
    God's altar is not in the sanctuary but in the world,
    and who seeks to make his or her sacrifices to God
    by way of the altar of a fellow person's need.
And all of God's children are disciples and servants
    and ministers.

2.

We often relish the comparatively easy pronouncements
    and promises of our Lord—
    those that comfort and pamper and make us feel
    happy and secure,
    and relegate the hard sayings to the realm of
    obscurity or misinterpretation.
But they don't go away—those hard sayings—
    and they demand a response.
They are the very words of our Lord,
    words like "turn the other cheek"
    or "go the second mile,"
    or the injunction that we first go
    and be reconciled to our brother or sister
    before we bring our gifts or offerings to God.
It means essentially that unless we do everything possible,
    even the giving of our lives,
    to bring love and light to the racial issue,
    and sustenance to the poverty-stricken,
    and freedom to the enslaved,

and justice to the oppressed,
we can hardly expect to continue worshiping God
with a pure conscience.
Maybe others can twist Jesus' words to say something else,
but I dare not, for this is what they say to me.

I am often provoked, when I should be challenged,
by what has been called the parable of the Great Surprise.
It is a parable of our Lord and is as great a surprise
to us today as it may have been in the
churches of the first century.
Judgment day is pictured;
the sheep are separated from the goats.
In which of the two groups do I belong?
Then comes the surprise:
"When I was hungry, you gave Me food;
when thirsty, you gave Me drink;
when I was a stranger you took Me into your home;
when naked you clothed Me;
when I was ill you came to My help;
when in prison you visited Me."
Then the righteous questioned:
"But when did we do this unto You?"
And Jesus replied: "Truly, I say to you,
as you did it to one of the least of these,
My brethren, you did it to Me."
And to those on His left hand, the goats, Jesus said:
"Truly, I say to you,
as you did it not to one of the least of these,
you did it not to Me."
Then Jesus concludes the parable by stating,
"And they will go away into eternal punishment,
but the righteous into eternal life." *(Matthew 25:31-46)*

My response is the question:
"Who, then, can enter the kingdom of God?"
Again, the answer comes from our Lord,

"With God all things are possible" *(Matthew 19:26 RSV).*
We have often failed to carry out the purposes of God.
Yet our great God never despises failures.
He redeems them, renews them,
    and recalls and reappoints them
    to ministry and servanthood.
This is what He is doing in us and for us even now
    in these disturbing and exciting end-times.

───── 3. ─────

It has always been assumed, and rightly so,
    that God's program for His church is evangelism.
Evangelism must always be the primary goal
    of the church.
It refers to the revelation of the good news
    of God's loving and reconciling grace
    to humanity all about us.
This has generally been interpreted as
    verbal proclamation or preaching.
There are places and times, however,
    where this method of communicating God's love
    to humanity is not necessarily the first most effective
    method of reaching our society.
Evangelism, if confined only to proclamation
    by preaching, is sometimes ineffective
    simply because most of the people on our streets
    already know what we are going to say
    before we say it.
After all, a twist of a radio dial can bring the
    proclaimed Gospel to them at any time during any day.
I have become convinced that our evangelistic efforts need
    to be recalled to, and recast about, that method of
    evangelism that was taught and demonstrated by Jesus.

Take, for example, the time when Jesus sent out the
   seventy disciples.
"I send you out as lambs in the midst of wolves,"
   He said, referring to their confrontation
   with an evil-infested, revolutionary world.
They were sent out two by two.
They were expected to place themselves at
   God's disposal and be guided by His Spirit.
Then they were simply to go out
   and share God's love with people.
They were to speak to people in an ordinary,
   friendly way, showing them their
   genuine concern for them.
They were to accept the hospitality of those whom
   they visited—
   to stay in one house, sharing their food and drink.
They were to be interested in and concerned about
   the people they visited,
   to accept them and seek to understand them.
They were to share themselves with these people—
   even to disclose their own needs and to accept
   what was given to them.
Then, when tensions were relaxed and the confidence
   of these people was won,
   their host would begin to reveal to them his problems
   and troubles, the needs of his household.
The host recognizes in these visitors a compassion
   and concern that calls out in him
   a responding spirit of trust.
After a relationship has been established,
   and the needs of the household and family become known,
   Jesus commanded His representative to
   "heal the sick there."
This may refer to whatever "sickness" or need that
   afflicted that household:
   a quarrel to be resolved, divisions to be reconciled,
   a deep-seated fear to be confronted and cast out,

some darkness or depression or anxiety or loneliness,
emptiness or purposelessness that must be dealt with.

The evangelists are commanded also to preach.
And their message is:
   "The kingdom of God is close to you—God is here!"
Their proclamation is of Jesus, by whose name
   they had been healing.
God has come into the world through Jesus Christ and
   stands ready to forgive and redeem, to set free and
   empower anyone who turns to Him and who accepts Him.

4.

Jesus went the way of the cross,
   offering up His life for our salvation.
He clearly predicted that His followers would have to
   go the way of the cross in order to advance His kingdom
   and accomplish His purposes in our world.
He wasn't referring to martyrdom only,
   but to the long-suffering and self-sacrificing that
   would be necessary in the process of communicating
   His love to His creatures throughout this world.
There is little cost involved in verbal witnessing.
There is pain indeed, and often much suffering
   in other forms of loving people.
God, through His Son,
   identified Himself with Him human creatures,
   sharing and bearing their pains and conflicts,
   embracing them in the midst of their failures,
   and drawing them into His eternal love.

This must be the style and pattern of our witness.
This is the way of Christian love.

It is costly because it involves a dying to self,
   a losing of one's life,
   and the discovery of life anew in the offering of
   ourselves to God in and through our fellow beings.
True, individuals may be
   converted by direct preaching or verbal witnessing,
   but probably these individuals have been
   previously prepared for just such a witness through
   the loving concern of others.
We must continue to witness—to preach—
   whenever the occasion arises,
   but our primary responsibility is to love—
   and to demonstrate that love in selfless,
   self-sacrificing ways—even if we are not always
   afforded the opportunity to preach.

Like the seventy disciples of our Lord's day,
   I believe that we, too, are meant to be thrust out,
   like lambs in the midst of wolves,
   into our secular and revolutionary world.
Our immediate purpose may not be to preach the Word of
   judgment or grace to those we meet.
We are to seek out those people to whom we can relate,
   who will respond to our friendship.
We are to share with them, listen to them.
When we have gained their confidence and they begin
   to share their pains as well as their joys with us,
   we are then to "heal the sick" or to use every means
   within our power and the power that God promises
   to meet those people and minister to those people
   at the point of their immediate and recognized need.
Our God may not transmit through us the power
   to heal diseases,
   but we do have the power to show love and concern,
   and there are resources within our reach to bring those
   people into contact with healing forces.
We can help to heal their loneliness,

to raise them out of despair, to restore their dignity,
   to help them find jobs or provide for some of the
   material needs that may alleviate their suffering.

We are always to seek to relate them to that One who is
   the answer to their deepest needs,
   to remind them that "the kingdom of God is
   near to them," that God is here.
To those fearful on account of their sins
   we can tell the good news that Jesus went
   to the cross on their behalf,
   that they can be set free from their sins and
   hangups and be guaranteed eternal life.
Through our love and concern we can channel to people,
   and introduce people to, the concern of the loving God—
   and to the power He offers to bring healing
   and enrichment, meaning and purpose, into their lives.
They have heard the message before;
   it probably meant very little to them.
Now, as never before,
   they see it demonstrated before them in our
   love and concern for humanity.
Now, as never before,
   they may be moved to accept it
   and respond to it.

———— 5. ————

We are not assigned or equipped to convert people.
That must be done by the Spirit of God.
It is our task to draw men and women to Christ.
It means that we *relate* to people,
   to reach people where they are,
   to communicate with them in the language

that they understand.
It means that we *involved* with their hopes
and needs, their strains and stresses,
their human and physical and material concerns.
It means that we *listen* to their joys and their agonies.
It means that we *love*—even at the risk of getting
our faces slapped or our knuckles rapped.
It means that we *respond* to the immediate needs of people
in our paths even when we know that their greater
need is something they still do not
understand or even anticipate.
It means that we *share*—our lives and possessions—
even when there are not visible returns
for our investments.
It means we must *proclaim* the power and presence of God
through Christ.
This is the ultimate purpose of our day-by-day mission,
even though it may take a very long time before
we arrive at that point with many of the people
with whom we deal.
And it is possible that we may never arrive at that
point with some people and yet may have prepared
them for the preaching and verbal witness
of others who will cross their paths.

Evangelism is our task; this is our method.
There are risks involved.
And we may never see the results of our witness to
some of those within our arena of responsibility.
But our great God never promised visible results,
only an open door of opportunity and the charge
to be faithful and obedient to our calling
as His ministers and servants.
We have been redeemed and empowered
to communicate the healing and saving love of God
to a distraught world.
Where there is hatred we must sow love.

Where there are wounds we must grant healing.
Where there is despair we must proclaim hope.
Where there is darkness we must shed light.
Where there is death we must proclaim life in Jesus Christ.
The grace of God has set us free to love.
And we are to love freely,
    knowing that the results,
    be they successes or failures,
    are in God's hands, not ours.

We Need the Commitment

Luke 9:57-62
Luke 14:25-35

1.

The key to contributive Christianity in
 these end-times is commitment.
I have been critical of what passes for Christianity
 in my circles of activity and influence.
The faith and fervor of the original Christians,
 the intense passion and power of those first
 followers of Christ,
 the devotion and drive manifest in the waking hours
 of the church are hard to come by in my generation.
The Christianity that I have been a part of is a kind
 of streamlined, plush-lined facsimile of the real thing.
It is too often a guilty conscience traded in for
 a soft cushion of comfort and consolation,
 or a kind of a defensive,
 crawling-into-our-holes-to-lick-our-wounds Christianity,
 an escapism, a running away from reality,
 a place of refuge and hiding.

This was not true of original Christianity,
    nor of the Christ of Christianity.
The soft faith that characterizes the religion of our day
    is not sponsored by Christ but is the invention
    of the minds of men and women who want the pearl
    without paying the price.
Even our Lord was tempted to settle for something less
    than genuine commitment.
It was a temptation to which He never yielded.
There was often a crowd following Him—
    mostly out of curiosity,
    seeking signs and miracles.
He persisted, however, in sifting those crowds and He
    discouraged lighthearted adhesion.
Thus He often turned and faced the multitudes
    and with a steady hand drenched with cold water
    the too easily kindled flame.
And then He would give them plain statements of the
    painful consequences that would befall those
    who followed Him—knowing that such would not
    quench genuine enthusiasm or love for Him.

We have, in our generation,
    inherited and possibly supported
    a vast array of cubbyholes and cults that
    specialize in some narrow aspect or incident of
    Christ's life and ministry—
    healing, tongue-speaking, forgiveness, deliverance,
    heaven, comfort, peace, eternal security—
    but which never embrace the whole Gospel
    or really follow the Christ.
Even salvation by faith, as valid and vital as it is,
    has become a sort of cubbyhole that limits the
    Christian experience to something intensely
    selfish and restrictive.
The alternative is not salvation by works,
    but the kind of faith that results in commitment

to those works that advance God's kingdom
and transmits His love and healing
to our disjointed world.

———— 2. ————

Our Lord consistently preached for commitment.
He never allowed or expected that His followers
    would get by with anything less.
And it was this kind of preaching that limited His
    following to a mere handful of publicans and fishermen.
When the crowds pressed in upon Him following
    His feeding-the-five-thousand miracle,
    He tried to tell them what it really was all about—
    that He was the Bread of Life and only those who
    identified with Him and His purposes would ever
    know the real meaning of life.
They left Him in droves.
Even many of our generation who should know better,
    consign His "eat my flesh" and "drink my blood"
    analogy to weekly Communion services and assume
    that such fulfills their obligations to be identified
    with and committed to the Christ.

When a young man,
    held spellbound by our Lord's miracles and messages,
    enthusiastically declared his willingness to follow
    Him wherever He would go,
    Jesus refused to sign him up and instead informed
    him that it would cost too much—
    more than he would be willing to pay.
There was no compromise in our Lord's approach
    to the rich young ruler.
"Ever since I was young I have obeyed all these

commandments," the young man said.
"You still need to do one thing," responded Jesus.
"Sell all you have and give the money to the poor,
   and you will have riches in heaven;
   then come and follow Me."
It is not surprising that this man never became
   a part of Jesus' entourage.

"You had better count the cost if you are going to
   be My disciple," said Jesus at one time or another
   during His ministry.
"My purposes for your life must take precedence over
   your country, parents, mates, children—
   even your very own life.
Indeed, if you are not willing to renounce everything
   you have,
   you simply cannot be My disciple.
Anyone who starts to plow and then keeps looking
   back is of no use to the kingdom of God."

Abraham was called to get out of his country and his
   father's house that he might be of use to God.
Moses was called to turn his back on those who brought
   him up that he might be free to serve God.
Jeremiah was commanded to deny himself the
   greatest joys of life, such as wife and children,
   in order to follow God's plan for his life.
It may wring our hearts to go contrary to the opinions
   of those we love,
   but this may sometimes be necessary
   if we are to follow Christ.
Our God may never call us to do what He expected of
   Abraham or Moses or Jeremiah,
   but whatever His word to us and His will for us,
   it is better that we make no decision at all to follow
   Jesus if that decision is to be a halfhearted one.

3.

I have faced up with Christ's total claims upon my life
    from the time I was taught about the Christian faith,
    but I read into those claims what I wanted them to say—
    or ignored them altogether.
Thus I have become a part of a tea-and-crumpets,
    country-club kind of Christianity that has no
    resemblance whatsoever to the pattern for discipleship
    that Jesus inaugurated.
I am living in the end-times.
It is time that I who call myself by His name throw
    out my adulterated concepts of discipleship and
    become authentic in my Christian life.
This necessitates my going back to His Word and
    pattern for my life.
There is nothing easygoing about the kind of life
    and committal that Christ prescribes.
It is costly and demanding.
It promises not softness but suffering,
    not comfort but challenge,
    not safety but sacrifice.
There is peace; there is also persecution.
There is security, joy, enrichment;
    there is also blood, sweat, and tears.

Our response to God's great gift of love
    and to Christ's call to servanthood
    must be commitment.
We can't be effective even in our secular goals
    and projects without commitment.
And yet all of those things are really only
    our avocation.
Our vocation is to serve God, follow our Lord,
    to be Christs incarnate in our world along with

    all our Christian brothers and sisters,
    ministers and servants of the almighty God.
And that vocation deserves and demands total commitment.
Of course there are risks involved,
    at least they appear to be risks in the
    three-dimensional world in which we live.
But the risk of being lost to God and His purposes
    is far greater for those who never move out of
    the cubbyhole of their initial spiritual experience.
Of course there will be failures in our determination
    to live committed lives,
    but there is always forgiveness and renewal when
    we fall and the grace to get up and try again.
And as committed Christians, maturing Christians,
    there is truth and life and order,
    purpose and objective,
    restoration and reconciliation.

May God grant to us the grace to respond to His love
    and live valid Christian lives in these
    end-time days of this dispensation.

On to Victory!

This chapter is the author's meditation on Revelation 19—22, reprinted from Prophets/Now, *copyrighted 1979 by Concordia Publishing House. Used by permission.*

This is not the time for despair;
    it is the time for celebration!
Jesus has come;
    He is present with us amidst the trials
    and tribulations of this tempestuous world;
    He is about ready to come again
    and to gather together His faithful followers
    into the fully revealed and eternally reigning
    kingdom of God.
The "marriage supper of the Lamb" is about to take place,
    and the suffering, celebrating, faithful children of God
    of all nations and generations are invited.
Christ will, once and for all time,
    reveal Himself as the living, overcoming, victorious
    Lord of heaven and earth.
Evil will be eradicated;
    all stumbling blocks will be removed;
    those who oppose God and His people will be overcome;
    the spiritual forces of evil will be bound and destroyed.
Sorrow will turn to joy, night into day.
Tears will give way to laughter;
    ugliness will yield to beauty.
Wars will cease and peace shall encompass people

      and nations, and all the world will recognize
      and give honor to the eternal kingdom of our Lord.
It is on this great day that the suffering martyrs,
    the struggling saints, the priests and prophets,
    servants and disciples of all the ages
    shall be united together to sing their praises
    to their eternal Savior and King.
Words cannot describe it—this fantastic event
    about to take place.
But God's faithful children—
    clothed in His righteousness—
    can believe it and hope for it
    and ready themselves for it,
    because it will happen,
    and all the pain and suffering
    that encompassed them in this world
    will be forgotten in the glorious
    revelation of Christ as King
    in the world to come.
Jesus is about to return and take His church to Himself.
He is coming soon!
Let us begin the celebration even now!